FOOD WE GET FROM THE LAND AND SEA

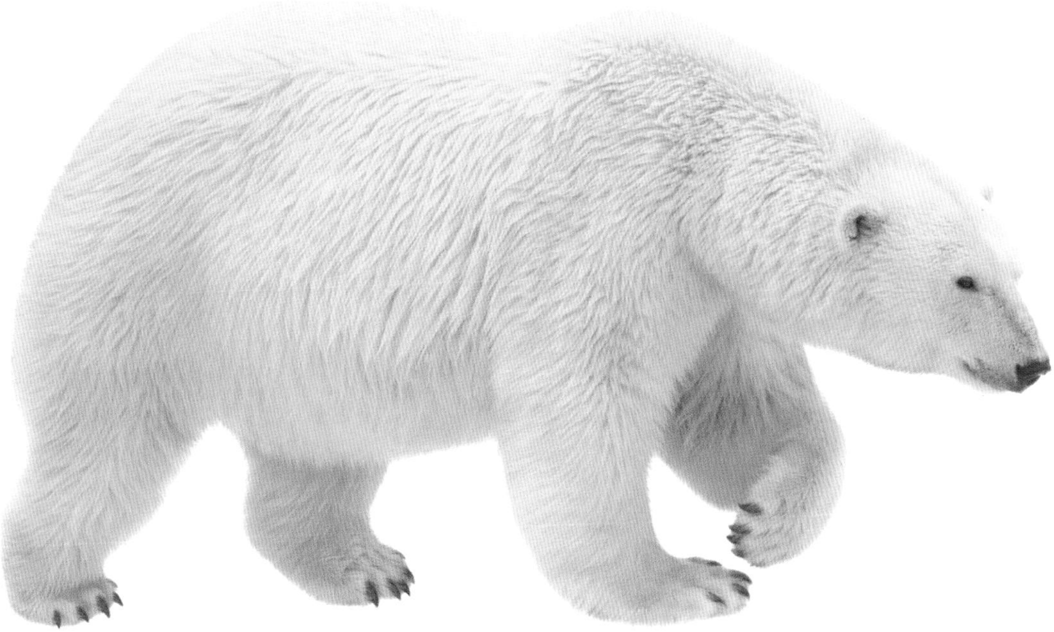

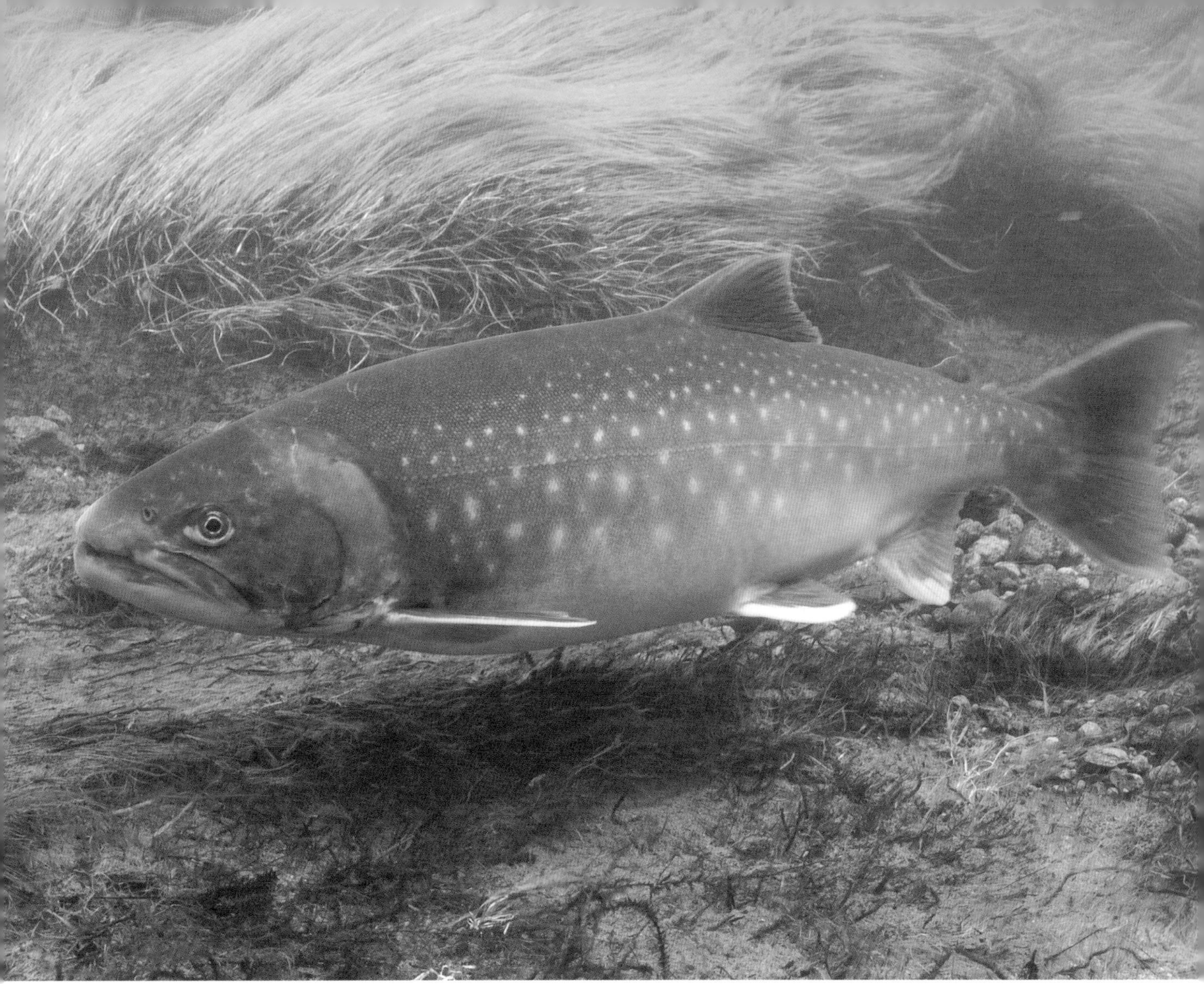

This is an Arctic char.

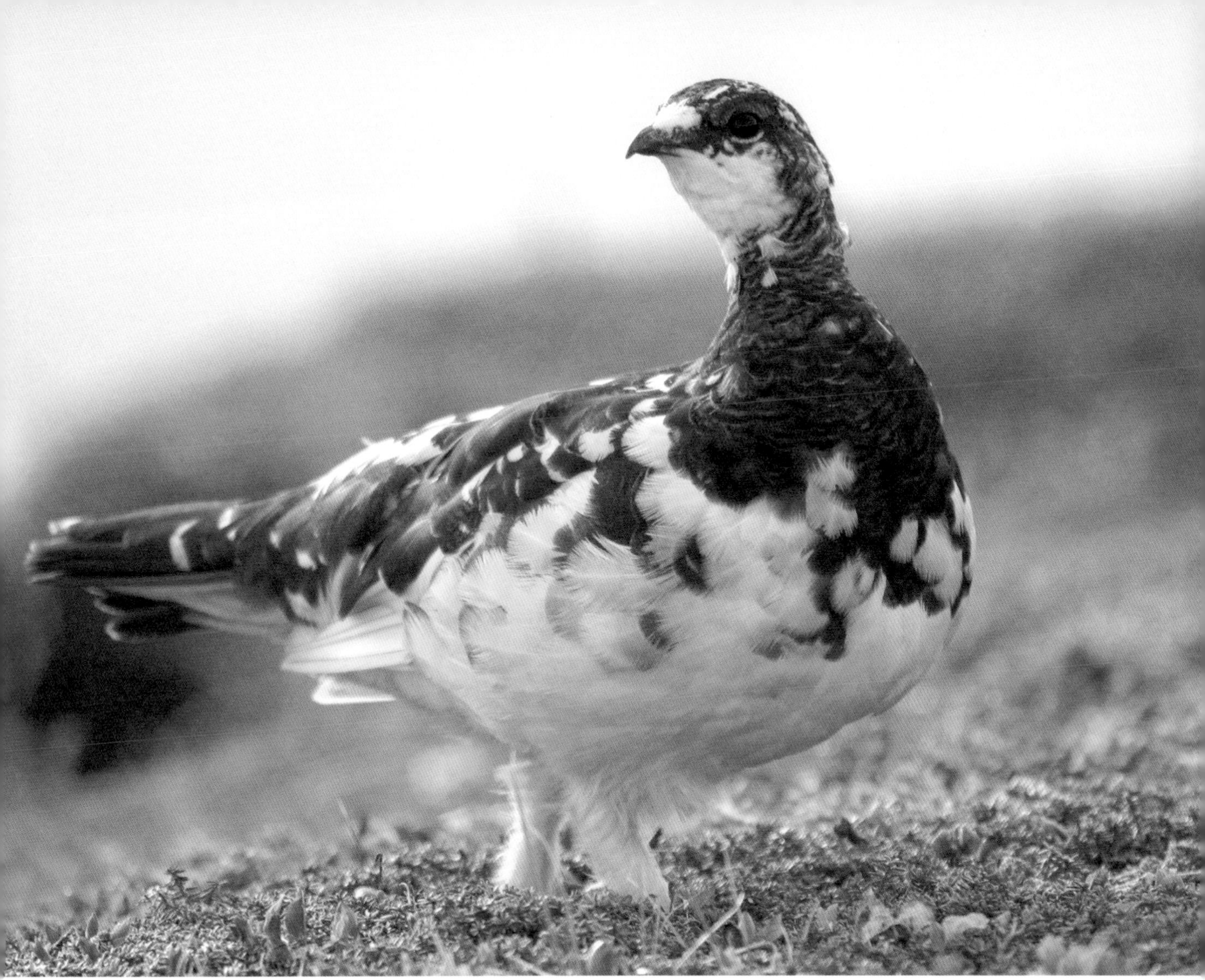

This is a ptarmigan.

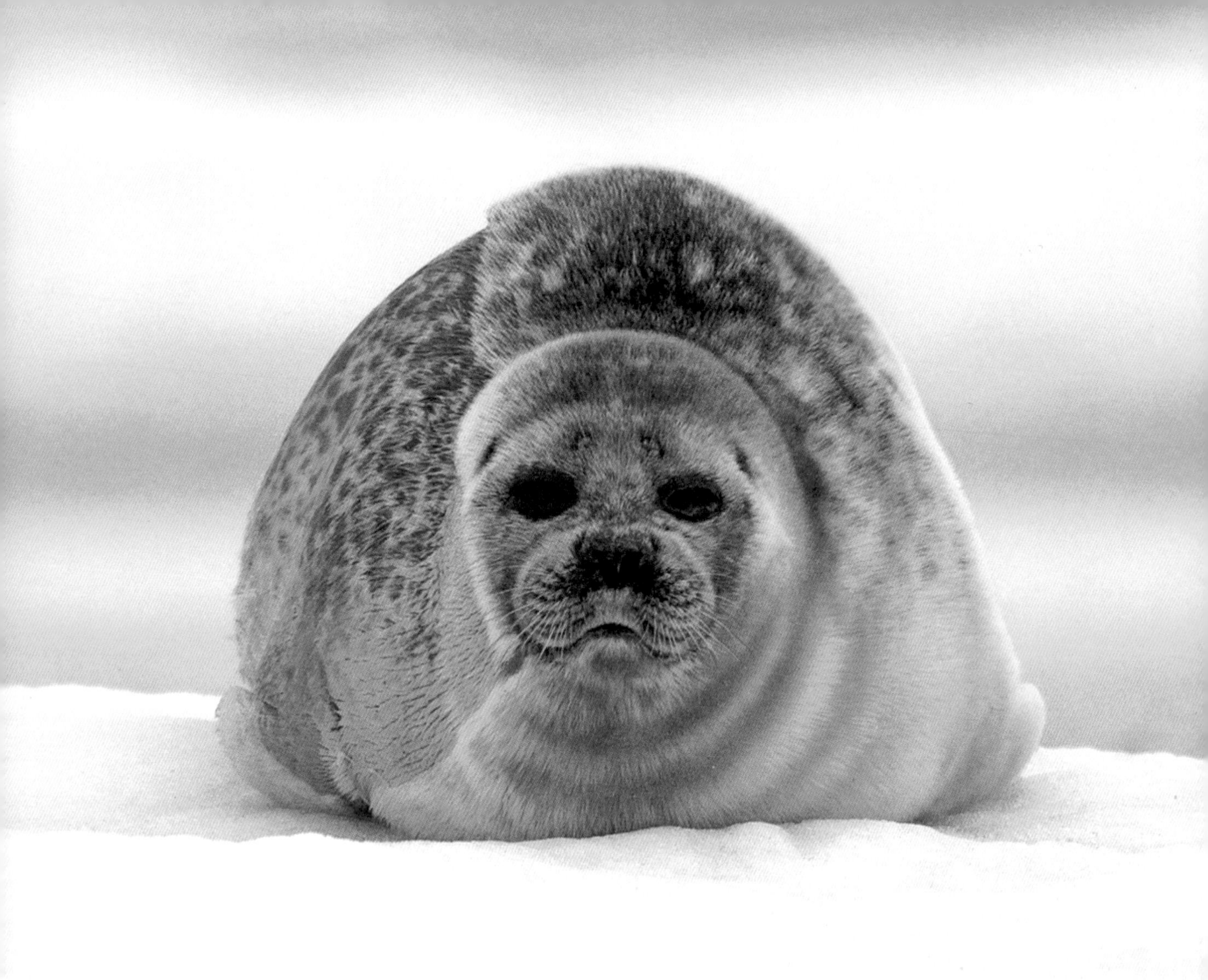

This is a seal.

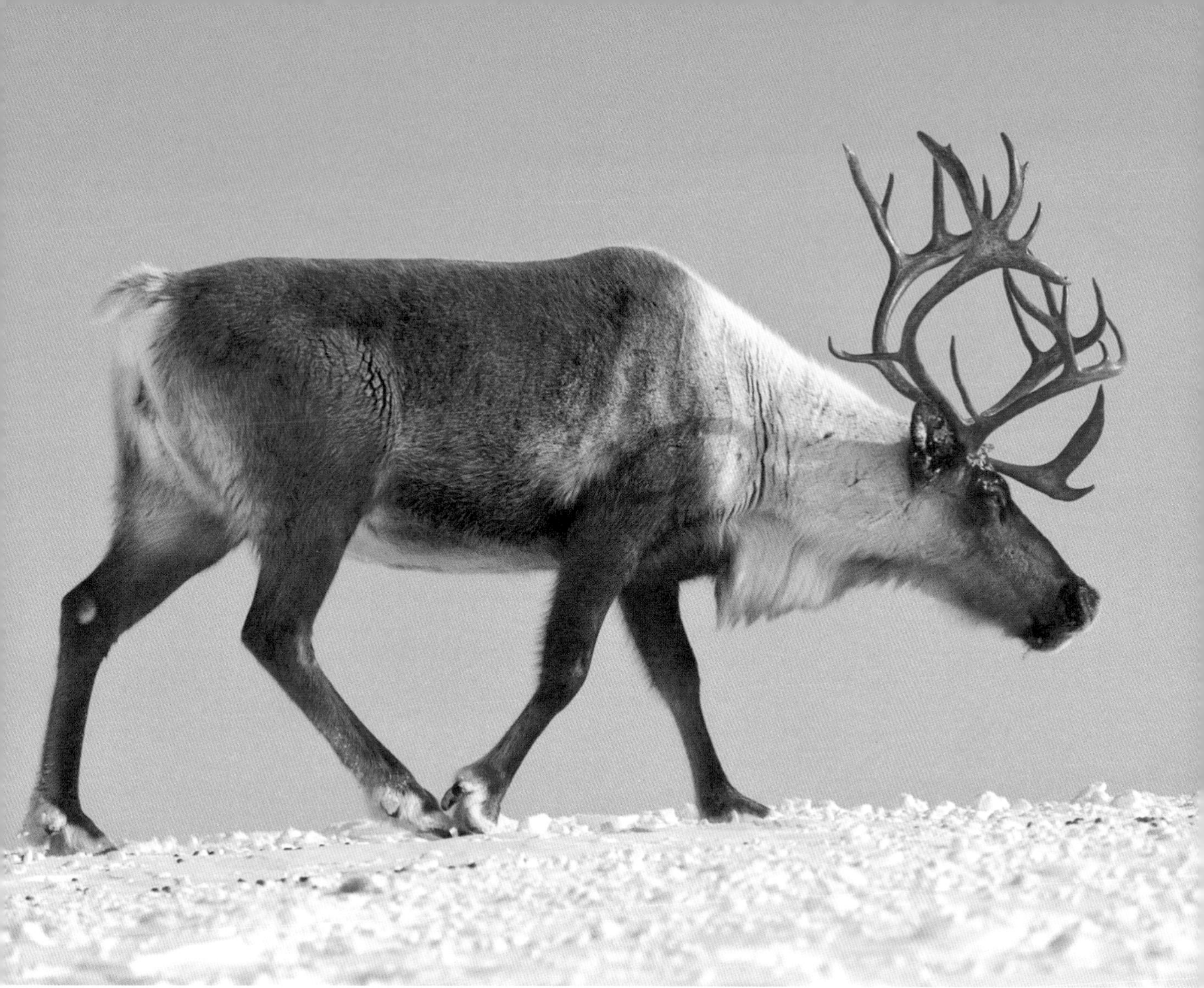

This is a caribou.

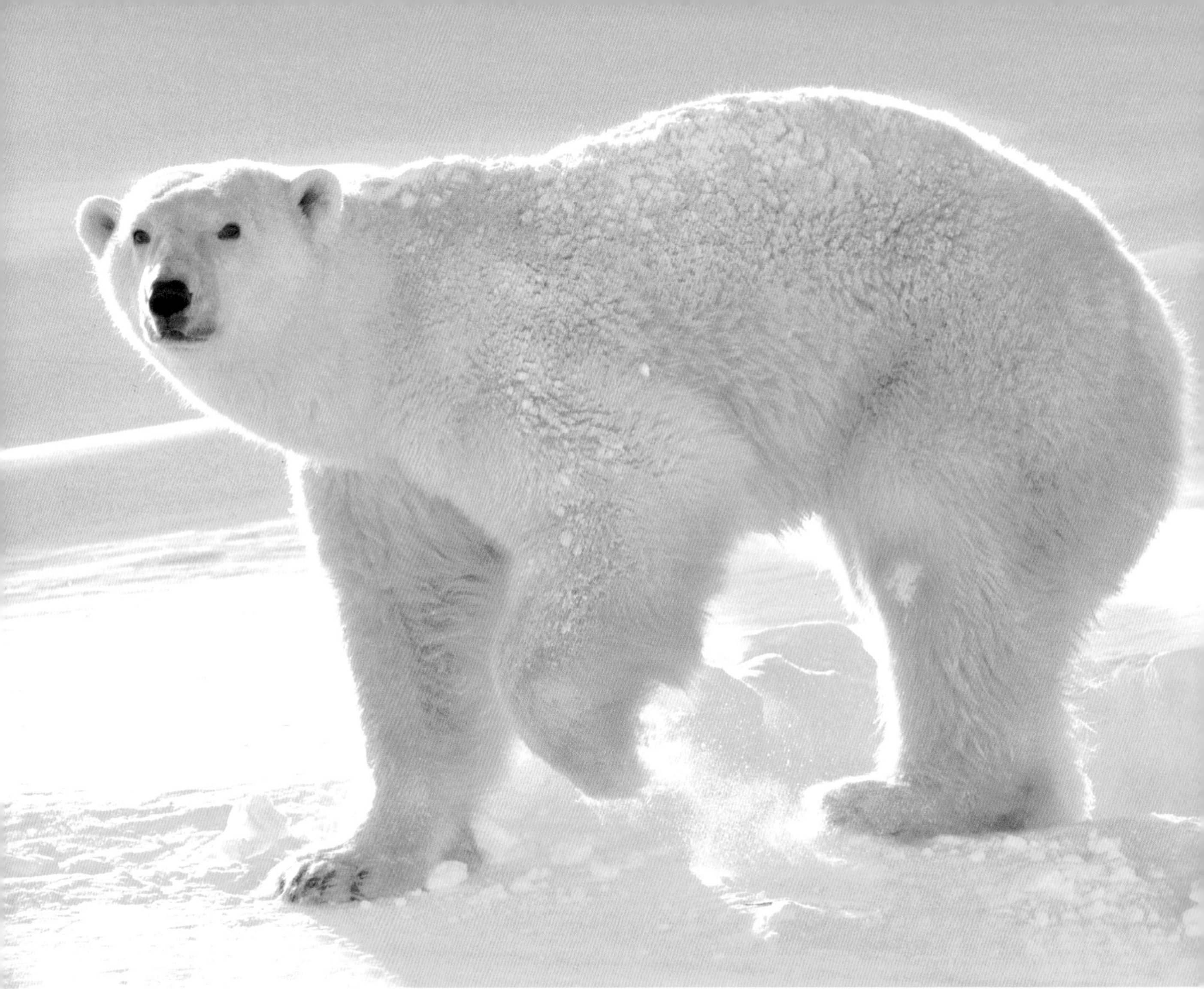

This is a polar bear.

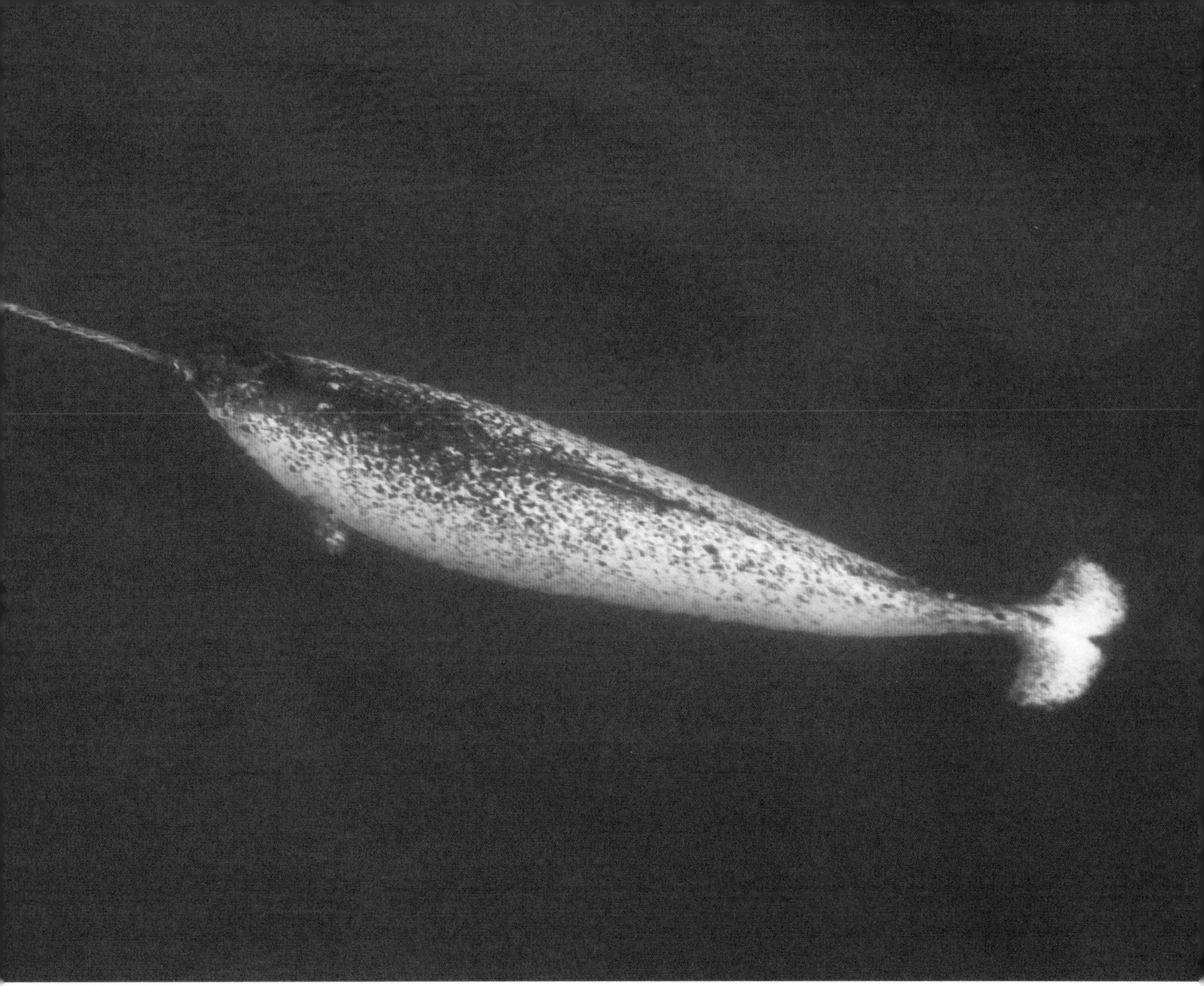

This is a narwhal.

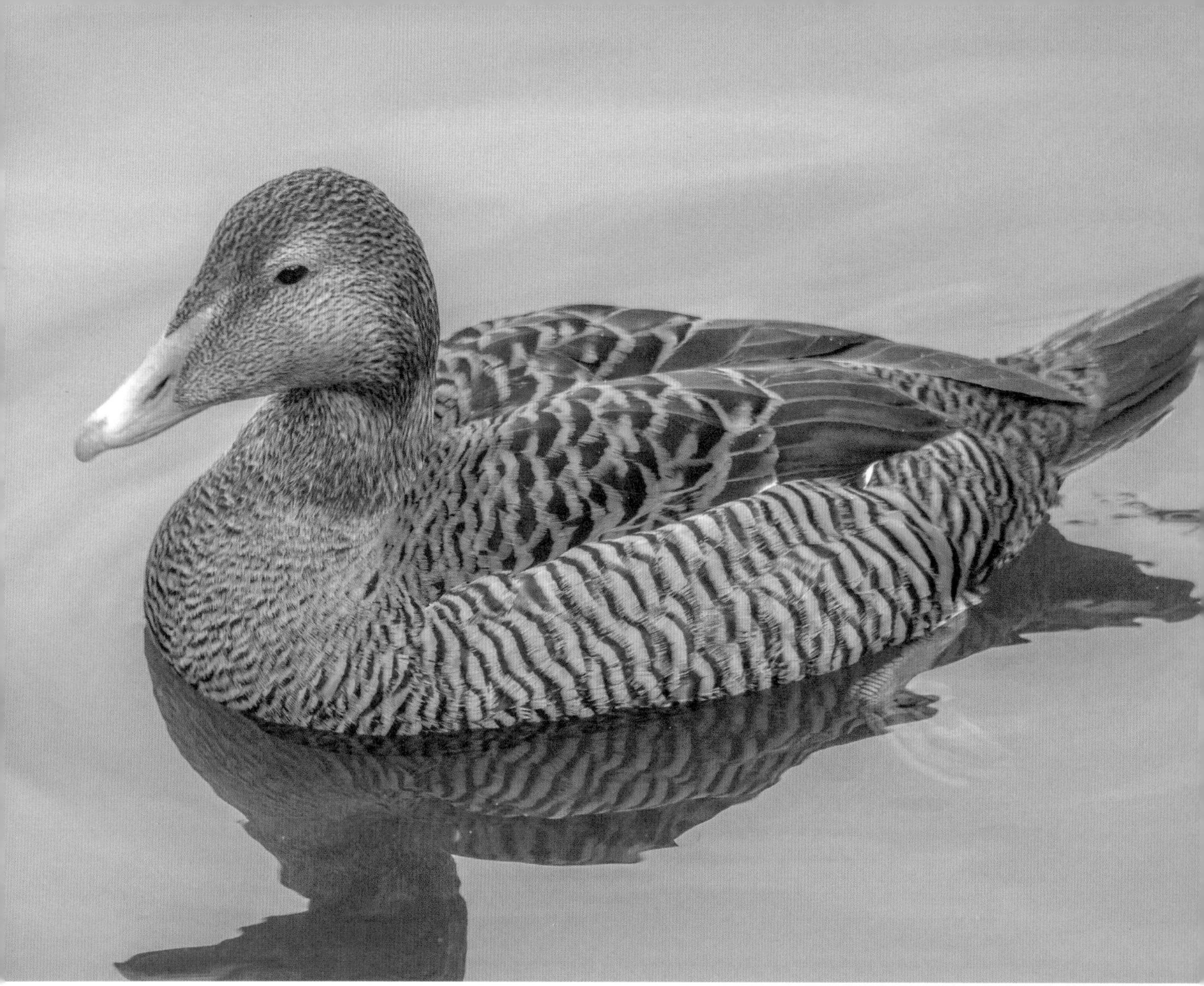

This is an eider duck.